Easter Bunny and Chick

(The Play)

Script by

Lance Bessey

ISBN 979-8-89345-348-5 (paperback)
ISBN 979-8-89345-349-2 (digital)

Christian Faith Publishing
832 Park Avenue
Meadville, PA 16335
www.christianfaithpublishing.com

Printed in the United States of America

Cast

Narrator
Mary
Joseph
Chorus
Shepherd 1
Shepherds (3-6)
Angel
Bunny (Fluffy white fur)
Bunny Family (Real or fake)
Baby Jesus (Real or fake)
Chick (Soft white plume)
Mother Hen (Real or fake)
Chick Family (Real or fake)
Crowd (As many as Director needs)
Three Kings
King Herod
Roman Commander

Roman Soldiers (As needed)
Roman Soldier 1
Roman Soldier 2
Boy Jesus
Bride
Disciples (3-9)
Peter (Disciple)
Disciple 1 (Disciple)
Disciple 2 (Disciple)
Jesus (man)
Crowd Member 1 (Crowd)
Crowd Member 2 (Crowd)
Crowd Member 3 (Crowd)
Judas Iscariot
Jewish Leaders (3-6)
Nobles (3-6)

Act 1

Scene 1

In front of closed curtains all on a darkened stage, Front Stage Left: Chorus sets. At Front Left Center: Stable with Mary and Joseph. At Front Stage Right: Pasture scene with Shepherds and their flock with Bunny family. Simple scenes that are easy to strike. Each scene will be on a darkened stage with spotlights to shine on active scenes.

Spotlights open on Stable Scene with Joseph comforting Mary within the simple stable scene.

NARRATOR: *(Microphoned in from offstage or set front stage left with chorus)* **Once upon a miraculous time at the very beginning, the virgin Mary and Joseph found themselves in a Bethlehem stable ready to give birth to God's chosen Son. His name would be known to all as Jesus.**

Spotlights remain on stable scene and open on chorus.

CHORUS: *(Sing **"Mary, Did You Know?"**)*

Spotlights fade from Chorus and Stable Scene and open on Pasture Scene with a shining bright light representing the radiating star over Bethlehem, which shines above on Stage Left.

Act 1

Scene 2

NARRATOR: Meanwhile, from a distance.

Shepherds are tending to their flocks of sheep in a night setting.

ANGEL: *(Appears from Stage Right as Shepherds cower in fear, and Bunny stirs from sleep)* **Hark! Do not be afraid! I am sent from Abba above to bring you the good news. The Messiah, your Savior, has come! You will find Him as a newborn baby wrapped in cloth lying in a Bethlehem manger.** *(Points to shining Bethlehem Star above Stage Left)*

BUNNY: *(Awakened wide-eyed and curious with the Angel's presence. Thinking out loud.)* **Wow! This must be something quite special!**

SHEPHERD 1 AND BUNNY: *(In unison)* **I must see this baby Savior!**

Shepherds pack up provisions and slowly walk toward the shining Bethlehem star Stage Left.

BUNNY: *(Hopping along trailing Shepherds)* **I am NOT going to miss out on being a part of this huge and important event!** *(Looks back for one last glance at the abandoned flock, possessions, and his family. Waves.)* **Goodbye. I'm going to make you proud.**

As the Shepherds and trailing Bunny make it over to Far Stage Left, Strike Scene settings while darkened, and the Bethlehem Star moves to Above Center Stage, and the Shepherds and Bunny shift and slowly walk toward Center Stage.

Act 1

Scene 3

NARRATOR: The trek was long and grueling, but finally, the exhausted yet thrilled traveling band of Shepherds and Bunny had finally arrived at this chosen city, Bethlehem, which radiated beneath the beaming, welcoming star.

Curtains open to Stable Scene Center Stage with Mary and Joseph kneeling next to Baby Jesus in His crib. Mother Hen settled with her chicks are set up far Front Center Right. The Shepherds with Bunny behind have moved to Center Stage Right behind a gathered crowd.

BUNNY: *(Squeezing through the thrilled yet exhausted Shepherds to the back of the crowd in front of stable)* **This may be a lowly stable to some** *(gesturing to Shepherds)***, but this** *(gesturing to stable)* **is a huge luxury suite for a worn-out bunny! Let's see if I can make it to the front to see this wonderment of a baby.**

(Bunny tries to wriggle through the crowd to the front, but the commotion of the crowd keeps thwarting his every move. Bunny gets bounced back to the rear of the crowd and Shepherds. Gasping with exasperation.)

Oh boy! This is exhausting! I better find a safe place to rest before I get trampled on.

(Looks around and spots Mother Hen with her chicks Front Stage Right, and Bunny cautiously approaches the nest. Chick seems to be encouragingly inviting Bunny in.)

Hello and thank you for welcoming me into your warm nest. Have you seen this baby Jesus?

CHICK: *(Shakes her head "no")*

BUNNY: *(Exhausted and nodding off to sleep)* **I must see this miracle baby…** *(Nods off to sleep just as the three kings arrive through the crowd and present their gifts of gold, frankincense, and myrrh at the foot of the crib)*

CHORUS: *(As Kings enter, sing **"What Child Is This?"** The lights fade as the song ends. Clear set of all but Mary, Joseph, Baby Jesus Stable Scene and Mother Hen, Bunny, and Chicks in their nest.)*

Act 1

Scene 4

Stage lights are dimmed, and there's a yellow spotlight creating a glow over Baby Jesus' crib.

BABY JESUS: *(Cooing from crib)*

Stage lights brighten on Hen's nest and Bunny.

BUNNY: *(Wakes abruptly cups ears toward cooing noise from crib. Shakes off sleep and focuses on yellow glow emitting over Jesus's crib. Gasps in wonderment.)* **Ohhh…magnificent… There's Baby Jesus.**

CHICK: *(In awe as she, too, is staring at Baby Jesus)* **Peep!**

BUNNY: *(Startled by Chick's peep)*

Both Bunny and Chick slowly turn their heads toward each other, and their eyes meet. Both quickly identify each other and slowly redirect their gaze toward Baby Jesus in the crib. Baby Jesus extends His hand from the crib and gestures Bunny and Chick to come over to Him. Bunny and Chick slowly move closer as if magnetically drawn to the crib.

BUNNY: *(Awe struck whisper)* **Finally, I get to meet this miracle baby that I've traveled so far to see.** *(Bunny and Chick draw closer with full focus on Baby Jesus)* **What is this magical force that pulls me closer?** *(Bunny and Chick reach crib)* **What is this**

shining yellow warmth that shines within? Just look at this amazing radiant baby…Jesus.

Baby Jesus reaches out and strokes both Bunny and Chick, and at His touch, a bright yellow patch appears on Bunny's white fur and Chick's white plume. This yellow patch remains permanently via Velcro or costume design.

BUNNY: *(Looking at his new yellow-patched marking and glancing at Chick's. Chick does the same.)* **Wow! This is Jesus, and He truly is the Messiah and true King that the angel professed Him to be!** *(Chick nods with utmost approval)* **I…err…we…** *(looks to chick and chick nods approval again)* **vow to follow and serve You always!**

The yellow spotlight glow radiates brighter, and then all lights dim and black out. End Scene and Act 1.

Act 2

Scene 1

Scene opens Front Stage Right in front of closed curtains with a quick palace setting with King Herod on his throne. Narrator is set on Front. Chorus in place Front Stage Left.

NARRATOR: There was a very jealous and dominating earthly king, Herod, who ruled over the Jews and had ties to Rome's rulers. *(Spotlights open on King Herod on his throne looking pompous)* **Herod didn't understand that Jesus merely wanted to have rule over people's hearts, including his; He didn't want to replace King Herod, but He wanted to lead him and all to a greater place.**

KING HEROD: *(His look of pompousness turns into a look of confusion, concern, and with troubled heart)*

CHORUS: *(Sing "I Can Only Imagine")*

KING HEROD: *(Troubled with hardened heart)* **What is all this stir about a newborn King? How dare anyone think they can threaten my crown and kingdom! I will have none of this!** *(Commanding to Offstage Right)* **Commander, come!** *(Commander with Soldiers rush in obediently from Stage Right. Commanding.)* **Hmm…this King** *(begrudgingly)* **Jesus, you say he's about two years old now?** *(Commander nods)* **I want you to hunt down children of all the land around age two and kill them!** *(Commander and soldiers obediently with adrenalin* *storm off Stage Right)* **That should put some fear back into my rule!**

End Scene. Stage lights dim and blacken.

Act 2

Scene 2

Scene opens in front of closed curtains and a spotlight on Narrator, if live.

NARRATOR: With the help of God's protection through the acts of others, Mary and Joseph left Bethlehem with their young boy, Jesus, to settle in the city of Nazareth and escape the evil, murderous plot of King Herod. Along with them, the family brought their newly adopted pets, Bunny and Chick.

Spotlights capture: From Offstage Left, a Child Jesus, Bunny, and Chick enter playing a child's game such as tag, leapfrog, tumbling, or playing around. They quickly exit Stage Left in flow of their game.

NARRATOR: Jesus's parents knew that Jesus was blessed with powerful gifts from God above, but it was when their boy was twelve that they began to witness Jesus's power and first miracle.

Center Stage wedding reception scene with a crowd in a tent, Bride and Mary are engaged in private conversation, and Boy Jesus at their side. Center Stage Left is a supply room including barrels of water, emptied wineskins, and a ladle.

NARRATOR: The first miracle occurred when Jesus's family was invited to a friend's wedding.

Curtains open to wedding reception scene. Bunny and Chick sneak in from Offstage Right.

NARRATOR: **Of Course, Bunny and Chick snuck in uninvited through a tear at the base of the wedding reception tent.**

BRIDE: *(Frantically to Mary)* **Oh, Mary, we're already running out of wine to serve our guests. This is devastating and really embarrassing. Our family reputation and honor are in serious jeopardy if we can't come out with more wine.** *(Pleading)* **Do you happen to have any or know where we can get some?**

MARY: *(In earnest sympathy for Bride)* **Oh no. I'm sorry, dear friend, but we're all out of wine. I don't know of anywhere to find wine at this late time.**

BRIDE: Oh my, oh my! We're going to be doomed with embarrassment. How will we ever get through this? We'll need some sort of miracle!

MARY: Miracle? *(Slowly turning head toward Jesus)* **Miracle… Son, Jesus, please help.**

BOY JESUS: *(Hesitant and contemplating this being His first miracle yet sensitive to the situation. Grabs Mary by the hand.)* **Come.** *(He leads Bride and Mary to Center Stage Left supply area. Bunny and Chick follow close behind.)*

BOY JESUS: *(Looking up and praying to Heaven)* **Please, Father, with Your power and will from above, allow Me to turn this water into wine.** *(Takes ladle, dips it into the barrel of water, and brings up ladle filled with rich wine. Violet drops shown by colored spotlight fall downward from the ladle and land atop Bunny and Chick to create a permanent patch of violet in symmetry with the patch of yellow. Jesus looks down upon them and smiles.)*

BRIDE: *(Relieved with great emotion and thrill, she embraces Mary and kisses Boy Jesus on the cheek as others look on.)* **Oh, what a true blessing and miracle! Thank you, Jesus!**

Curtain closes. Lights out.

NARRATOR: *(If available, video footage of various miracles projected on a screen would enhance this moment)* **The making of wine from water miracle was a beginning that opened up many more miracles created by Jesus as He grew and developed into a young man. Miracles ranged from curing the sick, casting out evil spirits, cleansing leprosy, healing the paralyzed, deaf, and blind, and even bringing the dead back to life. All these miracles through Jesus were credited to the power and glory of our Heavenly Father. Bunny and Chick were faithfully there by Jesus's side and were totally humbled and amazed by each miracle occurrence.**

CHORUS: *(Sings **"He Turned Water into Wine"**)*

End Scene.

Act 2

Scene 3

Scene opens with a massive crowd gathered with Jesus centered on higher ground or rock preaching the gospel with His disciples, Bunny, and Chick close by at Center Stage.

NARRATOR: Because of Jesus's powers, miracles, and attraction, huge crowds began to follow Jesus and His disciples. These crowds wanted to witness and be a part of this gospel and might that Jesus had been enlightening the world with. Right along with them were Bunny and Chick, just as they had vowed to follow Jesus all the way through. On the shoreline this day, the mass of crowds was thick.

DISCIPLE 1: *(With great concern)* Jesus! There are just too many people. We need to send them away for we cannot feed them all! We have no food!

DISCIPLE 2: *(Concerned)* Yes, Teacher, we must turn this crowd away. Otherwise, they're going to get angry and turn on us.

All Disciples bicker in panic among themselves and Jesus. Bunny and Chick look on with worry.

JESUS: *(Gives a reassuring smile to Bunny and Chick as they seem to sigh with relief, and next, Jesus turns to the Disciples with reassuring confidence and a smile)* Don't worry, my dear brothers, our Father above will provide and take care of those who are following in faith. Now, bring me all the food that we

currently have. *(Disciples hurriedly scurry about and bring back their gathered food)*

JESUS: Well, what did you come up with?

DISCIPLE 1: *(Gathering the food portions from the rest)* **Well, LORD, we've merely five loaves of bread and two fish. No way can we feed this mob of five thousand men.**

DISCIPLE 2: *(Double-checks the crowd)* **That's not even counting the women and children! Please, Lord, for the sake of getting mobbed, let's just call this a day and send the people home.**

JESUS: *(Again with a reassuring wink to Bunny and Chick and a reassuring gesture to His disciples, Jesus lifts the basket of rations toward heaven. As He lifts the basket into the air, two silvery-indigo flakes from the fish spotlight color fall upon Bunny and Chick where permanent patches of indigo burst in symmetry with the yellow and violet patches. Looks down at them and smiles knowingly.)* **Thank you, Father, for this food. Please, Abba, provide meals for this gathered crowd who meet in Your name to hear Your word.**

The Disciples gather around with empty baskets, and Jesus breaks up the food and evenly places the portions into each of the Disciples' baskets. You may use anywhere from three to twelve Disciples for this. The Disciples continue to walk around the setting delivering food from the same baskets. The crowd is eating in delight and having indistinct conversations occasionally spotting Jesus and nodding with approval. Jesus walks around greeting and indistinct conversing with the crowd with Bunny and Chick following and listening intently.

NARRATOR: Jesus greeted, addressed the crowd's needs, and He enlightened the crowd with God's word. The people all ate until they were satisfied. Finally, the time had wound down,

and the crowds left to return to their homes *(Crowd starts to slowly exit Stage Left and Right, and the Disciples begin to clean and gather the food baskets),* and the disciples cleaned up the mess before turning in themselves.

Lights dim, and the curtains slowly close as the audience views the crowd exiting and the disciples cleaning and gathering food baskets. Jesus enters Center Stage in front of the curtains with a spotlight on. Next, Disciples enter from Stage Left and Right, with baskets in hand. Scene strikes and sets behind the curtains.

DISCIPLES 1 AND 2: *(All Disciples eagerly and astonished approach Jesus with baskets extended)* **Jesus, LORD Jesus! Look! Look!**

DISCIPLE 1: *(To Jesus, amazed)* **It's amazing! The impossible has been made possible! It's a miracle!** *(Opens arms to include all Disciples)* **Look, LORD, we have twelve full baskets of food left over, yet we only had two fish and five loaves of bread to begin with!**

All Disciples nod agreeingly as they look at the baskets, Jesus, and each other in awe.

JESUS: *(Embraces His Disciples)* **Nothing is impossible with faith in our Father.** *(Looks up to heaven)* **Thank you, Father, our Provider.** *(Readdressing Disciples)* **Now, it's late, go ahead and sail to the other side of the sea, and I will join you on the other side. Please take Bunny and Chick with you. I want to be alone for now to pray.** *(Disciples obediently exit Stage Right with Bunny and Chick, and Jesus with folded arms to pray exits Stage Left)*

CHORUS: *(Sings **"Five Loaves and Two Fishes"**)*

End Scene.

Act 2

Scene 4

Center Stage Right Boat on the Sea at early dawn scene: The Disciples, Bunny, and Chick are all leisurely sailing along.

DISCIPLE 2: *(Startled and in fear)* **Look! There's a ghost coming at us from the sea!** *(All the disciples clammer about in fear with indistinct chatter among each other. Chick cowers behind Bunny and peeks ever-so-cautiously from behind.)*

JESUS: *(From across Stage Left and walking on water. Hollering aboard.)* **Take courage! It is I. Don't be afraid.**

The disciples in excitement with dismay as they scramble and rush to position themselves in better view of this sight. Bunny and Chick scurry to a safe corner of the boat in fear of being trampled.

PETER: *(Caught up in the rush and thrill, crawls out of the boat and starts to walk on water to Jesus, who's drawing closer from Stage Left. All other disciples are astounded and buzz with chatter, gasping, and pointing)* **LORD Jesus! I'm coming.** *(Just prior to reaching Jesus, Peter starts to look back at the boat and sea removing his eyes off Jesus. He starts to sink with arms flailing.)* **Help!** *(Gurgling)* **Jesus…**

JESUS: *(Gathers Peter safely as He leads Peter back to the boat. Consoling.)* **Oh Peter, don't look away. Keep your faith.** *(Jesus assists Peter into the boat, and then He climbs aboard. Two blue drops of water shown with a blue spotlight splash down upon Bunny* *and Chick and permanently appear in symmetry with the yellow, violet, and indigo patches. Jesus looks down knowingly and smiles at His pets as His pets look on adoringly to Him)*

Stage Lights dim and blacken as the curtain closes. Spotlight opens on Narrator.

NARRATOR: Through all of Jesus's works, loving messages, bestowed blessings, healing, and unfathomable miracles consistently witnessed, Jesus gained much adoration from His followers. Jesus even faced the devil who tried to tempt Jesus with every trick in the book to curse His faith in God. However, Jesus did not fail nor did He ever sin; Jesus lived a sinless life while here on Earth.

CHORUS: *(Sings **"Nothing Is Impossible—When You Put Your Trust in God"**)*

Lights dim. End Scene and Act 2.

Act 3

Scene 1

*Scene opens with JESUS, Disciples, Bunny, Chick, and a gathered crowd on Center Stage Right and the City of Jerusalem Center Stage Left. Jesus mounts a donkey (real or fake) as the crowd celebrates with chants "**King Jesus,**" "**Jesus our King**" as the Narrator speaks.*

NARRATOR: **It came time for Jesus to return to Jerusalem. He was coming back and declared King in favor of all the people. However, Jesus also knew that He was returning to danger as well. Jesus with His disciples along with Bunny and Chick arrived at Mount of Olives just prior to reaching the destination village. Jesus mounted on a donkey, which shows Jesus's humbleness as Servant and King, as He prepared to enter Jerusalem.**

*Jesus on donkey, Disciples, Bunny, Chick, and Crowd start to move from Stage Right to Stage Left toward Jerusalem. People from the crowd are laying down cloaks and branches in Jesus's pathway, chanting "**Hosanna to the Son of David!**" "**Blessed Is He Who Comes in the Name of the LORD!**" "**Hosanna in the Highest Heaven,**" and are buzzing with celebration and exaltation! This is all active as Narrator speaks.*

NARRATOR: **What a glorious sight it was to see as Jesus traveled into Jerusalem. An extremely large crowd had spread their cloaks, assorted branches, and palm leaves over the receiving street to pay homage to their arriving King. The people shouted.** *(Shouts from crowd on stage—see quotes above and wait for chants to subside)* **The crowd was a buzz with celebration**

and exaltation. *(Someone from Crowd waves a green palm leaf and places it at the foot of Jesus on donkey)* **Just as Jesus on donkey and His sidekick pets, Bunny and Chick, lay foot upon the first spread ceremonious palm leaf…** *(A green spotlight shines on Bunny and Chick's feet where it touches the palm leaf and a permanent green patch stays in place along with the already placed permanent colors. Jesus looks down and smiles knowingly and winks at Bunny and Chick, and they adoringly smile back.)*

Jesus and company keep moving from Stage Right to Left and parting through the crowd. Crowd indistinct chatter as to who is this Jesus with some nodding, some shrugs, and some shaking of heads in disagreement.

CROWD MEMBER 1: *(Gesturing to Jesus)* **Who is this?**

CROWD MEMBER 2: This is Jesus, the prophet from Nazareth in Galilee. *(Stir of commotion from differences of opinions same directions as above)*

CROWD MEMBER 3: Have you seen or heard of all the miracles Jesus has done? Jesus has got to be the Messiah, our Savior… our King!

NARRATOR: *(As Crowd continues to stir and commence in indistinct chatter of confusion, disagreement, or conviction)* **Now, this is where there was division in faith and belief that Jesus was indeed Lord and King. Some, since they had known or heard of Jesus growing up as a regular human being, found it hard to accept that Jesus was truly the Messiah. Others, who had faithfully witnessed all the wonderful blessings and miracles that Jesus had produced along with their belief in the written word of God, were total believers that Jesus was who He claimed to be.**

CHORUS: *(Sings **"I Don't Know How to Love Him"** as Jesus followed by Bunny, Chick, and Disciples meander through the crowd who continue with the above-mentioned reactions. Jesus is filled with love and truth for His people, Disciples are teaching and directing to Jesus, and Judah Iscariot is standing and conversing with Roman Soldiers who have arrived from Stage Left and look on.)*

As song ends, lights dim and black out, curtains close, and end Scene.

Act 3

Scene 2

Scene is set in front of curtains with front lights open. Jewish leaders are pacing and carrying on indistinct chatter with discontent and anger on Stage Right, and doing the same Stage Left are King Herod and Nobles. Jesus with welcoming, opened arms looks on. Narrator in place.

NARRATOR: With all the celebration that Jesus, the Messiah our King, had arrived in Jerusalem, the Jewish leaders and kings were angered, and they feared that their controlling powers and prestige would be lost. These leaders plotted to discredit Jesus in every way. However, every time these leaders challenged Jesus, Jesus would stand firmly to our Heavenly Father's will and words *(Jesus extends hands to Heaven)*, **and He would come out of each situation with even more believers and followers. Well, after Jesus performed numerous more healings and miracles while sharing His time and love with the people of Jerusalem, the time had come for the Jewish and Roman Leaders to do their treacherous deed.**

(Jewish Leaders cross Center Stage to join King Herod and Nobles on Stage Right, where they plot and all point and direct their attention to Jesus) **The devious plot involved one of Jesus's own disciples to set Jesus up to be captured by the jealous enemies.**

(Judas Iscariot enters Stage Left, shying away from Jesus as he crosses Center Stage to join the Jewish Leaders, Kings, and Nobles on Stage Right. Once with the group, Judah turns and points to Jesus. Jesus extends His arms knowingly to Judah with hopes that His lost sheep would reconsider his choice. Next, Jesus looks up

pleadingly to Heaven yet nodding in agreement and obedience) **Jesus, being the knowing Messiah and LORD, could have changed the gloomy situation, but this was God's plan and needed to play out.**

Stage lights dim and black out, and actors exit Stage Left and Right the way they entered. Jesus exits through Center Stage curtain. Scene ends.

Act 3

Scene 3

Scene opens with three lights out, blackened settings: Stage Center Right is set on a rocky mountain scene with Jesus's disciples asleep. Stage Center finds Peter within a city crowd. Stage Center Left holds Judas Iscariot with the Jewish Leaders, King Herod, and Nobles.

Lights open on the rocky mountain scene as Jesus, Bunny, and Chick enter from Off Stage Right.

NARRATOR: Bunny and Chick, being at Jesus's side all the way through as they had promised, witness many heart-wrenching moments of Jesus that came along with all the glorious times as well. *(Jesus, Bunny, and Chick approach mountaintop scene, shrugging and not understanding)* **Moments such as Jesus's disciples falling asleep in the midst of Jesus's sense of aloneness while struggling with God's plan. The plan that Jesus would have to leave His flock of loved ones here on Earth.** *(Jesus extends a questioning shrug up toward heaven, and next He looks for comfort in disciples only to find them asleep with a show of gentle yet frustrating disbelief)* **Also, that one disciple, Peter…** *(Lights dim and blacken on Mountain Scene and Lights up on Peter in City Crowd Scene and Jesus Bunny, and Chick approaching from Mountain Scene from Stage Right. Peter shies away from Jesus and tries to disappear into Crowd. Crowd members carry on with indistinct chatter, motioning, and pointing indicating that Peter is with Jesus.)*

PETER: *(Backing away from Jesus and bumping into first set of Crowd who are indicating with motions and indistinct chatter that he is with Jesus)* **No, I do NOT know him.** *(Bumbles away from first set of Crowd into another set of Crowd who are also motioning and indicating that Peter is with Jesus)* **No! No! I do NOT know Him!** *(Bumbles away into the third set of Crowd who are also motioning and indicating that Peter is with Jesus)* **No, certainly not, no, I do NOT know Him!** *(In realizing he had denied His LORD Jesus three times, Peter hangs his head in shame and gets lost in the crowd moving opposite of Jesus. Jesus looks longingly for Peter.)*

NARRATOR: Peter publicly denied Jesus three times before the rooster crowed after, just earlier, Peter vowed to fight for Jesus and to never leave Jesus's side. *(Lights dim and blacken on the city scene as Jesus, Bunny, and Chick move Stage Left from the city scene to Judas with authorities' scene. Lights up on Judas with authorities' scene. As Jesus, Bunny, and Chick approach, Judas Iscariot quickly approaches and embraces Jesus. Next, Judas stands behind Jesus, motions for the authorities, and points to Jesus. The Jewish leaders, King Herod, Nobles, and soldiers come and escort Jesus with authority off Stage Left. Bunny and Chick follow in a state of concern as the scene dims and blackens. Spotlight still holds and follows the action. Bunny and Chick remain on far Stage Left, where Jesus had exited with the spotlight remaining on them)* **Finally, the betrayal of Jesus's disciple, Judas Iscariot, who delivered Jesus to the enemies that had plotted to capture and kill Jesus.** *(Curtains close, strike the three stage sets, and set cross-setting Center Stage. Bunny and Chick are still in front of curtains with spotlights on them. Narrator in place.)* **For the sake of poor Bunny, Chick, and all our sensitive-hearted ones** *(Bunny and Chick closing eyes, covering ears, trembling and gasping in fear, and cringing at the narrator's every spoken word)***, let's cut through the gore, torture, disrespect, pain, and mockery that Jesus endured from capture to being nailed on the cross**

to die a death such like a convicted criminal. There, Jesus, a sinless and innocent "man," was lifted on the cross and left to die.** *(Curtains open to Jesus on the cross scene amongst a crowd. Bunny and Chick rush through the crowd over to the base of Jesus on the cross)* **With weeping and tears** *(Bunny and Chick weeping and looking on to Jesus with love and intent)*, **Bunny and Chick fought their way through the crowd that was filled with mixed emotions and found themselves at the foot of Jesus's cross. It was about three o'clock in the afternoon, and a mysterious darkness was creeping in all over the land.** *(Stage lights dim resembling creeping darkness)* **A pair of blood droplets slid down off the brow of Jesus where Roman Soldiers had mockingly driven a crown made of thorns into His head, and the droplets dripped down toward the earth below.** *(Red spotlights starting at Jesus's head cascade down to the earth below and land on Bunny and Chick where a permanent red patch appears)* **Jesus's blood splattered atop Bunny's white fur and Chick's white plume, creating red patches instantly in symmetrical form with the yellow, violet, indigo, and blue patches with the green patches at their footing.**

JESUS: *(Glances down with a weary smile knowingly at Bunny and Chick. Takes a last breath of earthly distress, and then He looks up to the Heavens above and belts out)* **Father, into Your hands, I commit My spirit!**

NARRATOR: *(Through staging and technology, coincide action with the narrator's spoken words)* **At that very moment, Bunny, Chick, and the crowd were startled by the supernatural occurrences happening around them. A massive curtain hanging in the temple was ripped in two from top to bottom, the earth shook violently, huge rocks split open, tombs broke open, and the bodies of many holy people who had previously died were seen raising to life, appearing to many of the Jerusalem crowd. Bunny and Chick were frantically** looking among the rising ones, hoping to find their Master Jesus. It was not to be as their eyes caught a glimpse of Jesus's body being carried away.

Lights dim and blacken as thunder roars. Curtains close. End Scene.

Act 3

Scene 4

Scene opens with Opened-Tomb set on Center Stage Right, which is guarded by soldiers. Mary, Peter, selected disciples, and a small crowd who are trailed by Bunny and Chick are in position Center Stage Left. Angel is out of sight within Tomb. Narrator in place.

NARRATOR: Three days later, Mary and some followers, along with Bunny and Chick trailing behind, went to deliver spices, pay their respect, and check on the tomb of Jesus, a tomb that was sealed with a massive heavy stone and guarded by soldiers. They were astonished to find the heavy-stoned tomb opened, so they curiously entered to seek their Master Jesus.

SOLDIER 1: *(Frantically entering and exiting the tomb in search of Jesus or any clues to His whereabouts. Inspecting everything and everywhere. To other soldiers who are also inspecting, frantic, and confused.)* **What has happened? There's no body, it's an empty tomb!**

SOLDIER 2: *(Shrugs with confusion and alarm as are all soldiers)* **I don't know, I don't know. We were here watching all night, and nothing was heard nor seen** *(confirming with other soldiers who confirm)*, **right?**

SOLDIER 1: *(Still puzzled, but needing to act, directs other soldiers)* **Quick spread out and search for the body or any clue you can find** *(Soldiers scatter and exit stage from all angles. Commands*

Soldier 2 over.) **You must go report to the commander and nobles!**

SOLDIER 2: **But what do I report? How can I report something that they're not going to believe when I hardly believe it myself!**

SOLDIER 1: *(Exasperated)* **Just do it. It needs to be told. Tell them what you know.**

Mary and Crowd, with Bunny and Chick trailing, approach from Stage Left. Soldier 1 attempts to stop them but, in anguish and confusion, moves aside to ponder the situation but still watches out with careful eyes.

MARY: *(To Soldier 1 and astonished)* **Kind sir, what has happened here? Is Jesus's body inside?** *(Soldier 1 is speechless, shrugs, and meanders aside perplexed)* **Oh dear, I must see.** *(Mary enters and exits the tomb)* **He's gone! Jesus is gone! What have they done with Him!** *(In utmost disappointment and tears of sorrow)*

ANGEL: *(Appearing from the tomb and all on stage cower to the ground in fright)* **Don't be afraid! You are looking for Jesus who was crucified?** *(Crowd nods agreeingly)* **He is not here. Jesus has risen! Now, go everywhere, and share this news!** *(Angel disappears back into tomb)*

Mary, Crowd, Bunny, and Chick, dazed and filled with mixed emotions of fear, awe, and thrill, start to exit Stage Left. Jesus enters Stage Left to greet them; the crowd is elated and filled with joyful tears in Jesus's presence. Jesus greets and embraces them all. Lastly, Jesus lovingly pets Bunny and Chick and at the touch, an orange spotlight and a permanent orange patch appear on each touch to Bunny's white fur and Chick's white plume in symmetry with the other colors. Jesus looks down on His pets adoringly knowing; He smiles and winks.

CHICK: *(Feeling a powerful odd sensation)* **PEEP!** *(Brilliantly colorful Easter eggs with all the pets' patch colors—yellow, violet, indigo, blue, green, red, and orange drop from Chick onto the Stage)*

BUNNY: *(Looking amazed from egg to Chick and Chick to egg. Aside to the audience)* **Wow! Just look at these most beautiful eggs ever, and hey** *(inspects his and Chick's fur and plume)***, they match the colors of our patches, which came from Jesus, our Master's, touch! These glorious, magical eggs! These** *(pause)* **Easter eggs!**

NARRATOR: *(As Jesus and the adoring crowd, which gain in numbers from all Stage exits, move slowly across Stage Left to Right. Jesus is teaching, loving, embracing as the crowd receives with excitement, love, and joy. Random Children come and gather Chick's Easter eggs with joy and admiration. The crowd stops in front of the Tomb, which has a yellow glow from the spotlight.)* **Jesus encouraged His followers then, and Jesus encourages us now to set everyone's mind at peace with God's truth and word that He has risen. Yes, Jesus has risen! It is through our Messiah, Jesus Christ, that we, too, may rise to God's Kingdom for eternal peace, love, joy, and glory.** *(Curtains close as the crowd surrounds Jesus who has extended arms to Heaven in front of the glowing tomb)*

CHORUS: *(Sings **"Blessed Assurance"**)*

As Chorus sings, Easter Bunny and Chick enter from Stage Right, hiding Easter eggs and end up on Stage Left. Children enter Stage Right with laughter and thrill, gathering Easter Eggs and spot Bunny and Chick and excitedly chase after them. Bunny and Chick exit Stage Left, followed by the chasing children. Narrator pauses for action to subside.

NARRATOR: Easter Bunny and Chick share Jesus's power, love, and will each year by hiding and displaying Chick's colorful glorious eggs at Easter. Easter, the celebration of Jesus who died on the cross for our sins, and He has, indeed, risen!

Lights dim and blacken. End Scene and Act 3.

PASTOR/NARRATOR: *(Rainbow spotlighted or graphic arts overhead)* **Though you won't find Bunny and Chick in the actual history of the Bible other than possibly being among the animals within the lowly manger at Jesus's birth, we want to make sure that our center of focus during Easter is on the grace of our Lord Jesus, who died for our sins and has risen. It is only through our faith in Jesus that we, too, may rise to be a part of God's beautiful, perfect, peaceful, joyous, and loving Kingdom. This is the true joy of Easter. Oh, and as for the colors, they are the colors of the rainbow. The rainbow is a symbol of hope in God's covenant, promises, words, and power. The color of a rainbow, which you'll find on Bunny and Chick's patches and Chick's colorful Easter eggs, have biblical meaning as well. Yellow represents the wisdom that comes with knowing the truth in God's word. Violet represents God's mercy, such as the mercy of Jesus dying on the cross so that our sins are forgiven, and we may have a relationship with God. Indigo symbolizes a covering or spirituality, such as upon Jesus's death and resurrection, the Holy Spirit came within us so that God's spirituality is always covering and guiding us toward His goodness. Blue represents divinity and the unknown, such as the depths of the sky and oceans where God's power and presence are limitless. Green represents healing, such as all the miraculous healings in the name of Jesus, where Jesus heals our wounds, pains, addictions, diseases, and brokenness. Red stands for energy or passion, such as Jesus and God's passion for us. God's passion is so great that He sacrificed His only Son to die on the cross so that our sins are forgiven, cleansed, and forgotten. We are, again, perfect in God's eyes. Jesus's passion is that we all come together in unison as part of God's Kingdom. Finally, orange represents warmth, joy, and emotional strength, such as the true joy in knowing Jesus and**

the true riches of eternal love, peace, and happiness that we're promised by God's grace through faith in Jesus. This concludes our Easter presentation. Go in peace and joy, knowing that Jesus has risen and resides within you. *(House lights on)*

www.ingramcontent.com/pod-product-compliance
Lightning Source LLC
Chambersburg PA
CBHW040117150726
48005CB00013B/1750